DINOSAURS
OF THE ARCTIC

Nunavummi

The Nunavummi reading series is a Nunavut-developed levelled book series that supports literacy development while teaching readers about the people, traditions, and environment of the Canadian Arctic.

Published in Canada by Nunavummi, an imprint of Inhabit Education Books Inc. | www.inhabiteducation.com

Inhabit Education Books Inc.
(Iqaluit) P.O. Box 2129, Iqaluit, Nunavut, X0A 1H0
(Toronto) 191 Eglinton Avenue East, Suite 301, Toronto, Ontario, M4P 1K1

Design and layout copyright © 2019 Inhabit Education Books Inc.
Text copyright © Inhabit Education Books Inc.
Illustrations by Aaron Edzerza © Inhabit Education Books Inc.

Printed in Canada.

Library and Archives Canada Cataloguing in Publication

Title: Dinosaurs of the Arctic / written by Dana Hopkins ; illustrated by Aaron Edzerza.
Names: Hopkins, Dana, 1982- author. | Edzerza, Aaron, illustrator.
Description: Series statement: Nunavummi reading series
Identifiers: Canadiana 20190193611 | ISBN 9781774502655 (hardcover)
Subjects: LCSH: Dinosaurs—Arctic regions—Juvenile literature. | LCSH: Dinosaurs—Arctic regions—
   Miscellanea—Juvenile literature.
Classification: LCC QE861.9.A68 H67 2020 | DDC j567.90911/3—dc23

ISBN: 978-1-77450-265-5

INHABIT
EDUCATION
BOOKS

DINOSAURS OF THE ARCTIC

WRITTEN BY
Dana Hopkins

ILLUSTRATED BY
Aaron Edzerza

Many different animals live in the Arctic today.
And long ago, dinosaurs lived in the Arctic.

Dinosaurs lived more than 65 million years
ago! Some were meat eaters. Some were plant
eaters. Some were big, and some were small.

When dinosaurs lived in the Arctic, it wasn't as cold as it is now. Back then, it was about as cold as the inside of a fridge.

Just like today, there was little or no sunshine in the Arctic in the winter. It was also cold and snowy. Dinosaurs had to be able to survive in these conditions.

UGRUNAALUK

One type of dinosaur that lived in the Arctic is the Ugrunaaluk. It had a bill like a duck and crests along its back. It had shorter front legs than back legs, but it walked on all four legs.

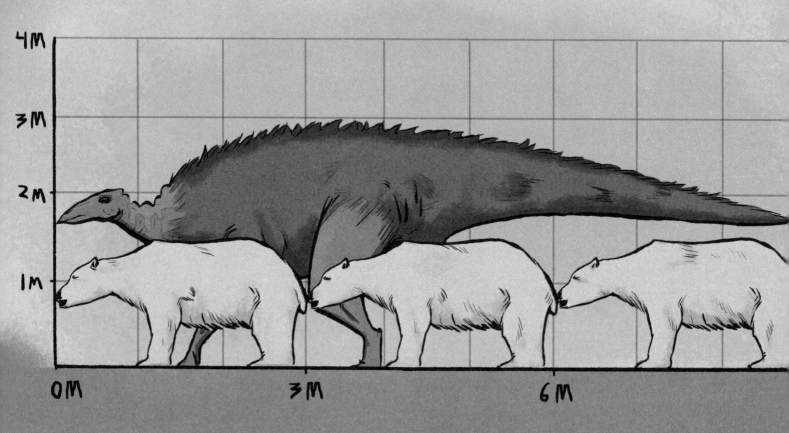

The Ugrunaaluk was 9 metres long. That's as long as three polar bears standing in a row! It was about 2 metres tall at the hip.

The Ugrunaaluk was a herbivore, which means it only ate plants. It ate twigs, branches, and fungi.

The Ugrunaaluk lived farther north than any other dinosaur discovered so far. The bones of the Ugrunaaluk have been found in Alaska and Nunavut, including areas in the very far north of Nunavut.

NUNAVUT

ALASKA

11

NANUQSAURUS

This is the Nanuqsaurus. Its name means "polar bear lizard" because it was discovered where polar bears live today.

The Nanuqsaurus was related to the Tyrannosaurus rex. It stood on its large back legs. It had sharp teeth and a long tail.

The Nanuqsaurus was about 6 metres long. That's about half the size of a Tyrannosaurus rex.

Scientists think the Nanuqsaurus was smaller because there was less food in the Arctic than where the Tyrannosaurus rex lived. Without as much food, the dinosaur would not have grown as big.

M

M

M

M

M

OM   6 M   13 M

The Nanuqsaurus was probably a carnivore, which means it ate other animals. Scientists think it had a very good sense of smell. It probably used its sense of smell to hunt.

The Nanuqsaurus lived in what is now Alaska.

PACHYRHINOSAURUS

This dinosaur is called the Pachyrhinosaurus. Its name means "thick-nosed lizard." It had a huge skull with a big, solid plate that stuck up above its forehead. It walked on all four legs.

Did You Know?

Scientists used to think that dinosaurs were a type of lizard. That's why so many dinosaur names mean "lizard."

The Pachyrhinosaurus's big plate is called a "boss." A boss is a thick bone on the skull. Some animals that live today have bosses. For example, the male muskox has a boss. It is where the base of each horn connects in the centre of the head.

The Pachyrhinosaurus lived in northern Alberta and Alaska. It was a herbivore, so it ate plants.

The Pachyrhinosaurus probably took care of its young, just like polar bears, caribou, and other animals do today.

ANKYLOSAURUS

Scientists have found bones and fossils of dinosaurs and other ancient animals in other parts of the Arctic, too. Fossils are remains of things that lived long ago.

In northern Russia, scientists have found fossils from an Ankylosaurus. The Ankylosaurus was a four-legged dinosaur that looked like it wore armour.

OTHER ANCIENT ANIMALS

Scientists have discovered other ancient animals in Nunavut. One is called Tiktaalik. This fish-like animal used its fins like legs to walk on the land.

There were also giant camels that once lived in the Arctic! Camel bones have been found on Ellesmere Island.

Scientists are only just starting to learn about dinosaurs and other ancient animals in the North. Who knows what other animals might have lived in the Arctic long ago?

Nunavummi

Nunavummi
Reading Series

The Nunavummi reading series is a Nunavut-developed levelled book series that supports literacy development while teaching readers about the people, traditions, and environment of the Canadian Arctic.

Level 10

- 16–32 pages
- Sentences and stories become longer and more complex
- Varied punctuation
- Dialogue is included in fiction texts
- Readers rely more on the words than the images to decode the text

11

- 24–32 pages
- Sentences become complex and varied
- Varied punctuation
- Dialogue is included in fiction texts and is necessary to understand the story
- Readers rely more on the words than the images to decode the text

Level 12

- 24–40 pages
- Sentences are complex and vary in length
- Lots of varied punctuation
- Dialogue is included in fiction texts and is necessary to understand the story
- Readers rely on the words to decode the text; images are present but only somewhat supportive

Fountas & Pinnell Text Level: M

This book has been officially levelled using the F&P Text Level Gradient™ Leveling System.